W9-BPO-456

MANAGING
WITH A HEART

Sharon Good

Sourcebooks, Inc.
Naperville, Illinois

Published by: Sourcebooks
P.O. Box 372, Naperville, IL   60566
(630) 961-3900
FAX: (630) 961-2168

Dedication

For the Light Group,
who always manage with heart.

Library of Congress Cataloging-in-Publication Data

Good, Sharon
   Managing with a heart : 205 ways to make your employees feel appreciated / by Sharon Good. — 2nd ed.
        p.   cm.
    ISBN 1-57071-125-9 (pbk)
    1. Employee morale. 2. Employee motivation. 3. Supervision of employees. 4. Personnel management. I. Title. II. Title: 205 ways to make your employees feel appreciated.
HF5549.5.M6G661996
658.3'14 — dc20   96-43218
                                                           CIP

Printed and bound in the United States of America.

10   9   8   7   6   5   4   3   2   1

INTRODUCTION

"Next to physical survival, the greatest need of a human being is psychological survival — to be understood, to be affirmed, to be validated, to be appreciated."

Stephen M. Covey
The 7 Habits of Highly Effective People*

Walk into almost any business today and the biggest complaint you'll hear is that employees feel they don't make a difference to the company — that is, they don't feel appreciated.

*A Fireside Book, Simon & Schuster, 1989.

With raises and promotions often precluded these days by economic conditions, job satisfaction and sup- portive work relationships have become paramount. Talented, hard- working people are leaving for other jobs, often because they don't feel their good work matters.

As a society, we spent the better part of the 1980s chasing the dollar. At the end of the decade, we found we were no happier and, in fact, that stress had become the greatest cause of our health problems. The advent of mind/body medicine has shown us the devastating effect a negative state

of mind can have on our physical condition. At a recent speaking engagement in New York City, Deepak Chopra, M.D., a physician/writer prominent in the mind/body health movement, listed numerous statistics to support this. The one that impressed me most, in the context of this book, was that one of the greatest causes of heart attack is...job dissatisfaction!

In light of this new information, and awakened to the importance of quality-of-life, we now want jobs and relationships that contribute to us — that make us feel fulfilled and joyous,

rather than diminished and depleted. And we're willing to put in the time and effort to seek out a situation that gives us those rewards. As business owners and managers, we can't afford to be constantly replacing good people who leave. We need to find a way to make our companies attractive and offer strong incentives to stay. One way to do this is to balance our concern for getting the job done with concern for the people involved.

In 1986, the U.S. Chamber of Commerce published the results of a survey: They asked employees what

they wanted from their jobs and asked employers what they thought their employees wanted. Employers thought their workers most wanted "good wages," "job security" and "promotions."

But number one on the employees' list was "appreciation," closely followed by "feeling in on things" and "help on personal problems." Clearly, employees are more interested in the human side of the workplace than the financial and prestige aspects. Morale on the job matters.

There are numerous examples of appreciation (or lack thereof) in action. For instance, a Buffalo, New York firm hired consultants to find out why employees from one division were applying for positions in another division — for lower salaries. They found that the supervisors in the first division were tough and inflexible about following the rules and had little compassion for their people's concerns. Those in the second division, however, always had their doors open to their staff and were much more forgiving about minor infractions of the rules.

The work in the budgeting department of a TV network was repetitive and tedious for the MBAs who worked there. But the director of the department gave consistent support to everyone — down to the typists — and rewarded the entire staff with expense account dinners for late nights and a department luncheon at the end of each budgeting cycle. Turnover in the department was almost nonexistent.

Employees are your greatest resource. Would you neglect your equipment and expect it to continue performing at its best? A computer

that isn't maintained will continually
break down. If its software is not
updated, it will not function up to
industry standards. An employee whose
needs, training and working conditions
are not handled will also fall into "dis-
repair." On the other hand, an employee
who feels taken care of on the job will
be focusing on work and not on finding a better job. Happy people are
healthier, more creative and more productive.

There are numerous people in
managerial and supervisory positions
who are responsible for other people's
morale. These include managers and

supervisors in business and retail, crew foremen and team leaders, head nurses or doctors, small business owners who hire a staff or engage freelancers, theatrical directors and producers, sales and team managers, those who deal with outside vendors or suppliers — even someone who hires a caregiver, housekeeper or plumber at their home.

As an employee, I've had the opportunity to hear my fellow employees (and myself!) grumble that they're not listened to, have no room to grow, are treated like they don't matter and numerous other complaints. As an employer, I've had the good fortune to

be able to do something about it.

This book offers a plethora of ideas to help you make your employees feel appreciated. They're meant to remind you of the value of your human resources, both as employees and as people, and that productivity is not separate from employees' well-being. They range from the conservative or "corporate" to the more playful or fanciful. Use the suggestions "as is," or let them spark your imagination to find ways unique and appropriate to your own company and personal style.

Some suggestions will be easy for you, while others will be more of a stretch or require more personal courage. If this whole concept feels uncomfortable or threatening to you, remember that no one is perfect — and that's okay. Just do your best. In the end, having happier employees will benefit you as well.

If you come across ideas you're already implementing, keep up the good work! But if you're reading this book, you probably feel there's room for improvement. Use the list and the examples to help you analyze where you may be falling short. Seek out

the methods you're not already using.
Let them inspire you. If you need more
help, there are dozens of management
and self-help books on the shelves of
libraries and bookstores. Or bring this
book to your own boss or manager
and ask for their help.

Since this book attempts to cover
a wide variety of work situations, not
all of the ideas will be applicable to
your particular situation. Companies
are structured differently and subject
to different rules and regulations.
Some are more formal or rigid, others
more casual or flexible. The President
or CEO will have a freer hand than a

middle manager. If an idea you favor needs the approval of your CEO — who doesn't agree with you — or is against company regulations, don't be discouraged. There are many items here that are based on principles of positive, supportive human interaction and communication that can be used in some form by anyone in any situation. Be creative and find ways in which you can enjoy working with your people that will encourage them as well.

Finally, I'd like to offer a heart-felt thanks to friends, family and all the people I've worked with over the

years — both as employee and employer — who have complained, confided, set examples and contributed ideas for this book and taught me what it means to manage with a heart.

Sharon Good
New York City

1

Go around and say "good morning" every day.

2

Get to know employees and treat them as individuals.

3

Learn their names.

4

Issue nameplates for desks or doors.

5

Give an assigned parking space. (Assign places randomly to avoid creating status.)

6

Remember birthdays.

7

Give them the day off on their birthday.

8

Remember their kids' birthdays.

9

Send a card for a birthday
or anniversary.

10

Give gifts for birthdays, weddings
and new babies. Throw a baby or
wedding shower, or a birthday
party.

11

Celebrate each person's anniversary with the company.

12

Give a get-well phone call or send a card to a sick employee.

13

When you go on a trip, bring back a small gift or souvenir.

14

Send flowers or fruit for family births, deaths and marriages.

15

Be concerned about their personal tragedies. A note saying, "Just to let you know your friends at X Company are thinking about you," can be very comforting.

16

Attend the wakes, funerals or shivas of employee families.

♥ ♥ ♥

17

Show employees that their ideas are listened to and make a difference to the company

18

Evaluate each person for who they are. If they're coming in 15 minutes late every day, but staying an hour late and completing the work well, don't get on their case about lateness. Some people need a little more flexibility.

19

Put out a suggestion box and
actually read the contents.

20

Give a "bright ideas" award for
great new suggestions.

♥ ♥ ♥

21

Use their ideas.

22

Give them credit for their ideas.

23

Send memos to let each staff member know you're thinking about them, that you notice what they're doing, their accomplishments, their difficulties, etc.

24

Send personal e-mail messages, such as, "Great job on the Acme report!" Encourage feedback via e-mail as well.

♥ ♥ ♥

"Appreciation raises self-esteem, self-esteem increases productivity...When you acknowledge someone for just being here, it can make a world of difference in his level of productiveness."

Mary Robinson
You are a Success!*

25

Videotape a message to your employees acknowledging them for their work, accomplishments, loyalty, cooperation — anything you want to thank them for.

*Heart Publishing & Productions, 1991.

26

26

If you have a TV or radio show, announce an employee's name on the air to commemorate a special accomplishment or occasion. If you edit or write for a magazine, mention their name in your column. Thank them when you accept an award.

♥ ♥ ♥

27

Let people know what, specifically, you appreciate about them, their work and their attitude.

28

On the completion of a job or project, say "thank you," of course, but don't forget to mention that the job was done well.

29

Be careful not to overcompliment
or do so insincerely — it wears
thin quickly and loses its meaning.

30

Create a pleasant, positive
atmosphere.

♡ ♡ ♡

31

Make sure the workplace is safe, attractive, comfortable and clean: good desk, chair, heat, air conditioning, lighting, kitchen, fire extinguishers and accessible, clean restrooms. Keep the walls painted, carpet vacuumed and desks and equipment clean, neat and in good working order.

32

Put up attractive pictures or inspi-
rational/motivational posters
(whatever suits the nature of your
business or employees best). If you
have a windowless office, put up a
picture of a window with scenery
or posters of scenery and open
spaces. Place flowers and plants in
strategic locations.

♡ ♡ ♡

33

Provide coffee, tea, bagels, rolls and juice as often as your budget allows (daily, every Friday, the first of the month).

34

If the company is large enough, set up an employee food service or cafeteria with reasonable prices. For a small company, set up a pleasant lunch room where people can get away from their work space for awhile.

35

Provide a place for coats and personal items, including a safe place to keep valuables, if necessary.

♥ ♥ ♥

36

Provide a company gym, masseuse, exercise or Weight Watchers classes free or at reasonable prices. Stress is our greatest health problem today, and addressing that issue would be a great way to demonstrate your appreciation in a tangible and very meaningful way.

37

If the workplace is cold and people are working with their hands, provide "Fagin" gloves — the ones with the fingers cut off — to help keep them warm.

38

If the environment is too hot or too cold, provide a personal fan or space heater.

♥ ♥ ♥

39

If the work is tedious, let them play a radio or Walkman to alleviate the boredom.

40

If you have a dress code, whenever possible, have a dress-down day. (Dress-down days have been proven to increase productivity!)

41

Create an atmosphere of safety and trust, not fear. People who are afraid of losing their jobs or being penalized for mistakes don't perform well.

♥ ♥ ♥

42

Bring newcomers around and introduce them to everyone. Be extra-attentive while they settle in and get to know people. Take them to lunch or have a "welcome aboard" tea for the staff. Supply a welcome packet with all pertinent forms and information.

A senior partner in an accounting firm known for low turnover and high morale had a boss who believed in loyalty to his employees. When she was going through a particularly difficult time with her teenage son, she made a mistake that cost the firm thousands of dollars. Instead of firing her, her boss assured her that he realized that the mistake was a lapse and that she was valuable to the firm. In the ensuing years, she returned his loyalty by turning down several very good offers from competitors, and her good work has made the firm considerably more money than it lost with her mistake.

43

Make sure newcomers are properly oriented. Show them the restrooms, cafeteria and supply room, and introduce them to relevant people. (That goes for consultants, freelancers and temps as well.)

44

Be careful not to treat temps like they're stupid or incompetent — remember that they're unfamiliar with your business.

45

If your employees are related to
you, as in a family business, treat
them with the same respect and
objectivity you would treat any
other employee. Be careful to
avoid favoritism, too.

♥ ♥ ♥

46

Hire the right person for the right job. Fit the personality and skills to the work. If you start out on the right foot, it'll be that much easier to be encouraging and show appreciation.

A congenial woman was hired for a sales position with a jewelry display dealer. The customers liked her and she worked hard, but she didn't have the aggressiveness or tolerance for rejection crucial to the position. She didn't do well. Her boss saw that she was struggling and, rather than lose a good worker, evaluated her strengths and weaknesses and concluded that she would be more suited to a back office position. Three months later, she was asked to replace the departing office manager. In the new position, she thrived and proved to be a valuable asset to the company.

47

Allow flexible schedules for valued employees with special needs (e.g., parents, those with multiple careers). Encourage part-timers, job sharing and working at home when possible. Be creative; don't get stuck in traditional modes.

48

Allow for creativity in getting a job done. Even if a project has been done the same way for years, a new employee may have some fresh insight.

49

As much as possible within the constraints of your business, allow your employees to develop their own work styles — provided, of course, the work gets done satisfactorily. If someone is just not a morning person and they can do their job just as well from 11 to 7 as from 9 to 5, let them. If someone needs to sit with a cup of coffee and a magazine for half an hour to collect their thoughts or germinate ideas, don't breathe down their necks — let them. Trust each person to be responsible for their job.

50

Give salespeople the freedom to be creative in meeting customer needs. It will make them feel useful and appreciated, and your customer service will be better as a result. Set limits if necessary.

51

Treat staff at least as well as you would like them to treat your customers. Show them what it feels like to have someone else be concerned about their needs. (You might want to read *The Customer Comes Second,* by Hal F. Rosenbluth and Diane McFerrin Peters.*)

*William Morrow, 1992.

52

If you see employees talking or kidding around and you know that they're always responsible for getting their work done, trust them and leave them alone! A few minutes of socializing can put one in a better frame of mind for work.

53

Allow personal phone calls and trust them not to abuse the privilege. Be clear about what the limits are (i.e., no long distance, no 900 calls).

54

Let them use the company car or service now and again for personal use.

♥ ♥ ♥

55

Treat everyone fairly and honestly.

56

Be clear about what you expect from your staff, trust them to do it, and acknowledge them when they achieve it. If they don't, restate what you want and discuss-where they fell short.

When a manager in a discount department store was promoted to operations manager, he thought the best way to make his mark would be to let everyone know what they were doing wrong so they could do a better job. He took copious notes and informed each person, politely, of his observations. He was confused when he began to notice people avoiding him, and was even more upset when he overheard an employee saying how much she disliked him. He took his problem to the district manager, who coached him to let people know what he expects of them, give lots of feedback and

praise, let them know what they can
do to improve and listen to them as
well. He implemented these suggestions and is now one of the most
respected (and well-liked) managers in
the district.

57

If you're not happy with someone's work, let them know why —
specifically — and give them a
chance to correct it. If you're still
not happy and must let them go,
see #165-166.

♥ ♥ ♥

58

If you've informed an employee that an aspect of their work is not acceptable and they correct it, let them know that they're on the right track.

59

Accentuate the positive — always remember to acknowledge the good work, not just point out the bad.

60

Let each person know when their
work or some aspect of it,
however minor, has improved.

61

Treat each person as if they were
successful in their jobs. See the
best in them, even when they
don't see it themselves.

♥ ♥ ♥

"Treat people as if they were
what they should be,
and you help them become
what they are capable of
becoming."

Johann Wolfgang von Goethe

62

If you see something going wrong, give constructive criticism — what the problem is and what can be done about it. If you don't know, come up with a solution together.

63

When you're the one who's made a mistake, admit it and take responsibility for it.

♥ ♥ ♥

64

Be a helpful older sibling, not a reprimanding parent figure. Let them know you're there to help, not to criticize or scold. Treat them as adults.

65

Don't dwell on past mistakes and failures. Forgive and forget and move on. If someone has the willingness and ability to improve, let them try without constantly reminding them of what they did wrong before.

♥ ♥ ♥

66

Give lots of encouragement —
you'll be amazed at the effect.

67

Remember that it's a two-way
street: bosses need to know you
appreciate them, too! Give positive
feedback and let them know where
you need more support.

68

If you are your own boss, take care of yourself, too. Make sure you have adequate help and support, and reward yourself now and then with a special lunch or some time off.

♡ ♡ ♡

69

Hire people you trust and allow them to do their job, giving them only as much guidance as they need. Nobody feels confident working with someone looking over their shoulder.

70

Don't forget humor. A little levity
can go a long way in lightening up
a situation and making people feel
comfortable. You don't have to be
serious to get a job done.

♥ ♥ ♥

A word processor at a small market research firm was paid a good hourly wage. She was responsible, her skills were excellent and she was capable of handling jobs that would have otherwise been farmed out to a much more expensive computer programmer or technician. But her boss watched over her constantly to make sure she was never idle and even told her he felt he was paying her too much. She began to doubt her own capabilities. Feeling angry after receiving no bonus one Christmas, she gave notice, leaving her work to a lower-paid, but less competent, co-worker. After doing temp work for several months, she was offered a position at an advertising agency, where her skills were appreciated and she was paid double what she had made at her old job.

71

Be a friend (but be careful to keep the business and personal aspects of your relationship separate).

72

Invite them home to dinner.

73

Give flowers "just because it's spring."

74

Write a song about them.

75

Show an interest in their personal lives. Ask about their kids, spouses, parents and pets.

76

Ask about the new house, car, stereo or computer. Send a house-warming gift.

77

Be nice to their family.

78

In a family crisis, give time off with pay.

79

Have a company psychologist
available to help with work and
personal problems.

80

Support their causes. Make a
donation or join a walk.

81

Recommend or share books, videos, movies and music that you like and think they would enjoy. Solicit their recommendations as well.

82

Order in coffee and cake some afternoon — just for the hell of it. Use the opportunity for you and your employees to get to know each other on a more relaxed basis.

83

Offer the firm's services or products for free or at a discount. If you're a carpenter, build them bookshelves. If you're an accountant, do their taxes. If you're a graphic designer, design personal stationery. If you're a lawyer... well, there are so many things you can do!

"You can run an office without a boss,
but you can't run an office
without secretaries."

Jane Fonda

84

Send flowers on Secretary's Day.

85

Send flowers not on Secretary's Day.

86

Take the team to lunch after the completion of a project.

87

Have a Christmas party or give everyone a turkey.

88

Throw a company picnic or sponsor a day at a local amusement park for them and their families.

89

Have a farewell party or luncheon
for a departing employee.

90

Let them take an extra long lunch
or leave early when things are
slow. During the summer, allow
them to leave early on Fridays if
their work is finished, or have
half the staff take off
alternating Fridays.

91

Whenever possible, manage projects so they're not last-minute, forcing employees to work late or under too much pressure. Last minute projects often do not allow people to perform at their best.

92

Make sure everyone has adequate
breaks, especially if the work is
physically or mentally demanding.
If one person takes a break while
others choose to forgo it, don't
penalize the one who
needs it.

♥ ♥ ♥

93

If an employee has put in a lot of overtime on evenings and week-ends (particularly if they're salaried and don't get extra pay), reward them with "comp" days (extra personal days), expense account lunches or dinners, or other perks, within your company's and legal regulations.

94

Don't ask an employee to do personal work for you. You might offer the work to them as an outside job that you pay for, but make it clear that they won't be penalized if they turn it down.

95

Remember that people have a life outside of work. Don't expect them to work late and on week-ends all the time. If the work is not getting done, get more help.

♥ ♥ ♥

96

Make sure your good people feel
supported. Just because they're
performing well doesn't mean they
don't need to know you're there.
A good person who feels ignored
will look for another situation
where they do feel appreciated.

97

Provide an adequate support staff for salespeople. Give them leeway to provide samples and incentives for their clients.

*T*he owner of a popular restaurant decided to branch out into catering. She hired excellent team leaders who loved their work and managed their teams efficiently. The catering business grew. As the owner became more involved in keeping up with the paper-work from two booming businesses, she began to neglect her team leaders. "They're doing a great job," she reasoned. "They don't need me watching over them." The team leaders began to feel the lack of support. Three of them decided to leave to form their own company. The owner found herself spending time replacing them. Within a few months, all of her top leaders had left for their own businesses or a competitor. The level of service declined and the catering business began to lose money. By the end of the year, it was closed.

98

If your company has multiple offices, send a Christmas card to the other offices with a picture of your staff and "who's who." It's always great to be able to connect a face to a name or a voice on the phone. If you find yourself in the vicinity of one of the other offices, drop in and say "hello."

99

Videotape meetings at headquarters and send copies to branch offices. Conduct an annual meeting at each site.

100

If you have employees working off-site, go down and see how they're doing — maybe even pitch in and help. Have someone at the site report to you regularly so that you're in touch with their working situation. Have a personal connection. Make sure they feel your presence and support.

♥ ♥ ♥

101

Go out on the road with outside reps. See what their day is like and what problems they encounter.

102

If someone is working in or around your home, find out what they like for lunch and provide it.

103

Find out what products your housekeeper prefers, what they don't like or are allergic to, and provide the best.

104

Treat housekeepers, caregivers and other home workers with dignity, respect and kindness. Remember: in terms of our humanity, we're all equal and have the same basic human needs and rights.

105

Give freelancers and temps extra work so they can qualify for their (union) health plan.

106

Bring in pizza for lunch and sit around talking about things other than business.

107

On a hot summer day, buy ice cream for everyone.

108

Be a mentor to a promising employee. Find out what their goals and dreams are. Guide and encourage them.

109

Help them move their careers forward. Post job openings and promote from within. Give people a chance. Assist them in planning a strategy for growth within the company or industry.

110

Pay for courses that will enhance professional skills (workshop, degree or certificate programs).

111

If they're having trouble with an aspect of the job, provide guidance or help. If it's outside of your abilities or of those in your company, bring in a consultant or enroll them in a course.

112

Ask for help when you need it. Pride only forms a barrier between you and your associates. A little show of humanity and humility will engender a closer working relationship.

113

Offer workshops in relevant areas, such as teamwork, public speaking, interviewing, writing, financial management, time management, conflict resolution and computer, presentation, leadership and management skills.

114

Send a note or greeting card of congratulations on a promotion.

115

The person who is the head of an
organization sets the tone (and
the standards) for that group. Be a
role model. Create a climate of
excellence, productivity and
positive reinforcement, and you'll
see it echoed throughout
your company.

♥ ♥ ♥

116

Have high expectations for and of them, and let them know that you know that they will succeed in meeting those expectations. Remember that you can empower them.

117

Instill a sense of company pride. Always put your best face forward. It feels good to be connected to a company you admire.

118

Foster cooperation rather than competition in your department, group or company — even between teams.

119

Be a colleague rather than a boss. Refer to your "associates" rather than your "employees."

♡ ♡ ♡

"Nobody starts a new job with a bad attitude. Companies create them. The rare company that can capture that 'first-day' spirit in its people and nurture it throughout their careers has learned the secret to exceptional service."

Hal F. Rosenbluth

President & CEO, Rosenbluth International,
Co-author, The Customer Comes Second
and Other Secrets of Exceptional Service*

*William Morrow, 1992.

120

Expect the best and trust them to produce it.

121

Sympathize when they're having a bad day. Even if you can't do anything to lighten their load, just knowing that you care will make a difference.

122

Work as a team.

123

When a project is up against a
deadline or in a crisis, don't go
home and leave your staff to do
the work or fix things — it
makes them feel resentful and
unsupported. If you pitch in, or
are at least available for questions
and encouragement, they'll be
much more willing to make the
extra effort to get the job done.

124

Teach them things, such as how to work better with a particular client or a more efficient way to approach the task at hand. Be patient if they don't learn as quickly as you expect.

125

Let them teach you things, such as how to use the equipment or a new skill they learned in a workshop.

126

Treat your associates like they work with you, rather than for you.

127

Work side-by-side with your team and learn what their day-to-day experience is like.

128

Hold regular team meetings to keep up-to-date on the project and provide support.

129

Invite teams to choose team or region names that inspire or excite them. "The Dynamos" is a much more empowering name than "Region 3."

♥ ♥ ♥

"The return from your work must be the
satisfaction which that work brings you and
the world's need of that work. With this,
life is heaven, or as near heaven as you can
get. Without this — with work which you
despise, which bores you, and which the
world does not need — this life is hell."

William Edward Burghart (W.E.B.) Du Bois

130

Be a good leader. Instead of being a boss, be a coach. Listen rather than talk. Support rather than criticize. Facilitate and guide rather than dictate.

131

Be accessible. Keep an open door during the day, and make your home phone number available for emergencies after hours.

♥ ♥ ♥

132

Include support staff (secretaries, word processors, assistants, mail room, interns) as part of the team. Be sure that they, too, are involved in the planning and acknowledged for the success of the project.

133

If you use the services of an outside agency, treat the agency personnel as part of your team, not like the enemy. After all, you do have a common goal.

An independent drug store was known for its excellent customer service. Although it was more expensive than the chain store down the block, many customers were willing to pay extra for the personal attention. In this store, the employees participated with the pharmacist/owner in the management of the store — the choice of products, shelf and window displays, hours, standards of service — and they felt tremendous personal pride in their work.

134

Don't forget yourself. Look in the mirror and tell yourself you've done a good job. Treat yourself to something special.

135

Take a management skills course or read a book.

136

Read *The One Minute Manager**
and implement it.

137

Listen to their complaints and let
them know that they matter to
you. Do your best to respond and
improve what you can.

*Kenneth Blanchard, Ph.D., Spencer Johnson, M.D., Berkley
Books, 1983.

138

Communicate honestly and openly.
Be willing to hear bad news as well
as good. Employees will be quicker
to forgive your mistakes if they
feel you're trying to communicate,
listen and respond.

13.9

If someone comes to you with a complaint (e.g., sexual harassment), take it seriously and give it fair and proper investigation.

♥ ♥ ♥

A systems analyst in a large corporation spent a year overhauling her company's proprietary software. She put in many hours of overtime and finished the job in the allotted time and under budget. When raise time came around, she was dismayed to receive only a small cost-of-living increase. Over the next few months, her manager noticed that she seemed unmotivated and reluctant to take on new responsibilities. What her manager had failed to communicate to her was that the company had put a limit on raises and that she was one of a handful of people in the company who had gotten any raise at all.

140

Respect their feelings. You're much more likely to get cooperation if you help someone work through their feelings about the job or a co-worker than if you demand that they "get over it and get on with the job."

141

Invite them to your office for a cup of coffee and a chat. Schedule one-on-one time for each employee (or at least key employees).

142

If two or more employees are not getting along, help them to negotiate their differences. Don't just leave them alone to fight it out — especially if it's work-related or affects their work. Listen to each person's story. Bring in an outside consultant or counselor if the problem is big enough or requires greater objectivity.

♥ ♥ ♥

143

Periods of transition (moving, restructuring, mergers, expansion, downsizing) can leave employees feeling insecure, uncertain and edgy. Let them know that you're concerned about their well-being during this trying time. The personal touch is best — drop by for a chat, or speak to them as a group. Let them know what's going on and that they can come to you or your staff with their concerns.

144

Take a survey of employee attitudes. Find out what they feel works and doesn't work about your organization.

145

Periodically do a tour of the facility. Have "town meetings" and let employees ask questions anonymously, on paper. Address their questions for the group.

♥ ♥ ♥

146

Employees like to complain about bosses. Don't give them reason. Implement an "open door" policy to your office. If they can come to you with their complaints, they won't have to go behind your back.

147

Give performance appraisals and feedback on a regular basis. It shows employees that they are respected and valued and that their contribution is important and recognized. It also gives a sense of security in that they know where they stand.

♥ ♥ ♥

148

Let them take part in their own
evaluations with self-appraisal
forms. Have them evaluate
you as well.

149

Let them write their own job
descriptions — find out what
they're really doing.

150

Keep everyone informed of developments on the job. It helps them do a better job and promotes good will — people who know or suspect that something is going on behind their backs get nervous and suspicious.

151

Conduct weekly meetings to keep
your staff apprised of the status
of projects, what needs to be done
and what's not getting done.
Include everybody. Keep them up-
to-date with calls, memos
or e-mail.

152

Let the people involved in a job develop the systems and procedures with you, rather than imposing your ideas or "established procedure" on them. Most often, the people "in the trenches" know the workings of the machinery better than the "generals," and you'll avoid ending up with something that looks good on paper but doesn't work.

♥ ♥ ♥

When new routes were added, the on-time performance rate at a regional airline dropped. The vice presidents, unable to remedy the situation, turned to their employees for help. They formed a group headed by a sky cap, a flight attendant, a pilot and a ramp agent, with a manager acting simply as a facilitator. Within two months, the performance rate was not only restored, but became the highest in the industry.

153

Spend a week or a month doing the jobs of the people you supervise to give you firsthand experience that will empower you in understanding and managing them.

154

Let employees review company policies and procedures and suggest changes based on what is actually happening. People are more likely to be responsible for and support policies they've had a hand in creating.

♥ ♥ ♥

A social work office in a small city hired a consultant to set up a computer system. Based on his work with similar companies, he set up new computers for each person, plus one laser printer and two draft printers to share. But the busy social workers never had time to print drafts. Instead, they often found themselves queued around the lone laser printer while the two draft printers remained idle.

155

When buying equipment and supplies, find out what's needed or would work best from the people who use them. Be sure that the complexity of the equipment matches the level of proficiency of the intended users.

♥ ♥ ♥

156

Provide the best possible tools (computers, machinery, vehicles, access to information, etc.) to allow your employees to do their best work. Remember safety when choosing equipment.

157

Even if you can't supply the best of everything, let them know that you would if you could.

158

If something in your company or a department is not working, put your energy into finding a solution rather than someone to blame.

159

Communicate without blame. Instead of "You forgot to give me the equipment list," try "I also need the equipment list."

♥ ♥ ♥

160

NEVER, under any circumstance, belittle an employee.

161

If an employee has made an error, instead of chewing them out, just state what they did wrong. If you know how to correct it, tell them. If not, work out a solution together.

162

If you have a high employee turnover, find out why. Ask questions, and be willing to hear the truth.

"It is easy — terribly easy — to shake a man's faith in himself. To take advantage of that to break a man's spirit is devil's work."

George Bernard Shaw
Morell in Candida

♥ ♥ ♥

163

Don't stand over people. If there's a better or more efficient way to do the job, teach them or offer suggestions, but don't treat them like they're deliberately wasting time (if they really are, that's another matter — see #57). Everyone has their own work style.

164

Conduct exit interviews. Find out why people are leaving. If there's a repeating pattern, find out why and make improvements.

165

Don't fire an employee without warning (unless, of course, you're forced to by unforeseen layoffs or budget cuts). Besides being unfair to that person, it scares other employees — if you can do that to one person, you can do it to anyone — and makes for bad morale and distrust. If you're unhappy with someone's work, give them a warning and time to correct it. And if ultimately you do fire someone, tell them why and give them a fair and appropriate severance package.

166

If you do have to fire someone, be gentle and compassionate — and don't do it around Christmas or their birthday.

167

If you hire someone who, it turns out, doesn't fit in well with your company, sit down with them and discuss the problem honestly. Chances are they feel as out of place as they seem to be, and you can come to a solution together — whether they stay or go.

168

Make sure the payroll is always on time — that check means a lot to people! (And make sure it doesn't bounce.)

169

When you give out checks, add a Post-It that says "Good job!" or "Glad to have you on the team!"

170

Give a special bonus other than at Christmas or year-end — for the completion of a special project or as a general incentive for good work.

"Highly publicized for paying wages considerably above the average, [Henry] Ford began in 1914 — the year he created a sensation by announcing that in the future his workers would receive $5 for an 8-hour day — a profit-sharing plan that would distribute up to $30 million annually among his employees."

The Columbia Encyclopedia
Columbia University Press, Fifth Edition, 1993.

*A*n accomplished salesman in a computer hardware company earned a commission of $30,000 one month, despite a lack of support from his home office and his boss's refusal to give him a car phone. As his boss handed him his commission check, he complained (as he did every month) about having to pay him so much, although the company had earned ten times that amount from his work. The salesman lamented his situation to a friend, who offered to submit him for a position in his company. With his excellent track record, he landed the position easily and left his former boss to rely on less experienced (and less productive) salespeople.

171

Give regular raises.

172

Give a raise before they ask for it or before it is due.

173

Give a bigger raise than they expect or are due.

♥ ♥ ♥

174

When you hire someone or
engage a freelancer, pay them
more than the going rate.

175

Pay them what they're worth, and
don't begrudge them the money
or make them feel they're not
worth it.

176

If you absolutely can't give a raise, explain the situation clearly and offer to create a new title or position. Trust them with new responsibilities.

177

Give the best benefits package you can afford. Offer profit sharing, contributions to pension programs, health insurance, a company store and discounts on company products.

♥ ♥ ♥

178

Provide a company doctor, especially if the work is high-risk or dangerous.

179

Give a reasonable amount of sick days, personal days and vacation days. Or just give a number of personal vacation days to use at their discretion.

180

Allow them to take "well days" in lieu of sick days. Taking off that beautiful day in June to play in the park will do wonders for their mental (and physical) health. Having that escape valve will probably allow them to get sick less often, and they'll take fewer days off (and be more productive) in the long run.

Set up day care for working parents. They'll be much more productive if they know their kids are in good hands (and if they can go by and see them during lunch or breaks). Pick up the cost if you can (all or part); if not, keep the cost as low as you can, perhaps by offering the use of an empty conference room or office and allowing participating parents to collectively hire a caregiver(s).

182

On business trips, stay in the same hotel as your staff. If they fly coach, you fly coach.

183

Don't blatantly shower yourself with a high salary, bonus, company car and other perks while your employees are receiving low wages and benefits. (In many companies in Japan, the top executives can only receive seven times what the lowest-paid employee receives.)

♥ ♥ ♥

184

Take a lesson from Mr. Scrooge —
if you get a windfall, share the
wealth. Don't just sock it away for
yourself — especially if the windfall was the result of other
people's efforts.

The manager of the word processing department at a liquor company received dozens of cases of liquor each Christmas as gifts from various department heads. Every year, his staff watched as he took it all home, never offering any to his supervisors, much less the operators. When a last-minute job came in on New Year's Eve, not one of his staff was willing to stay late to do it, and he was forced to turn the job in late.

185

Issue a Certificate of Achievement, Excellence or Appreciation for a special accomplishment. Offer awards for teamwork, customer service and greatest improvement / increase in quality, sales or service.

186

Award a pin for length of service or outstanding service or quality.

187

Award special privileges (e.g., executive cafeteria, use of the car service, use of the company apartment in London or San Juan, extra vacation days).

♥ ♥ ♥

188

Publish an employee newsletter to help bring the company (especially a big one) closer together. Print news about employees and events. Take classified ads. Do feature articles on one or more employees.

189

Feature them in the company newsletter.

190

Put a citation letter or recognition form in their permanent record.

191

Allow teams to set specific goals and give a reward when they reach them. Let them choose the (non-cash) reward, such as dress-down Fridays, a company-sponsored baseball team, a coffee-and-cake or lunch celebration, award certificates or plaques.

♥ ♥ ♥

192

Display samples of outstanding work.

193

For a reward or special occasion, give a gift certificate (some, especially men, prefer this to flowers).

194

Institute motivational / recognition programs. Give tee shirts, sweatshirts, beer coolers, keychains, mugs, coffee warmers, computer games, theater tickets, hats and frisbees (perhaps with a company logo) as a reward for quality work. The return in work will be worth the expense.

♥ ♥ ♥

Tie rewards to effort rather than the success or failure of a project when circumstances are out of their control (e.g., budget cuts, natural disasters, project cancellations).

A product manager in a drug company was given the job of preparing the launch of a new product that was awaiting FDA approval. His team worked for several months, only to find that the drug did not receive FDA approval and would not be introduced on the market. The Vice President overseeing the product called in the product manager and his team to break the news. He commended the excellent work they had done on the project and assured them that their bonuses would not suffer that year for a failure that was out of their control.

♥ ♥ ♥

196

Choose an Employee of the Month. Throw a luncheon or dinner and invite their family. Say nice things about them. Put their picture on the wall. Write them up for the company newsletter. Give a plaque. Give a bonus.

197

Let customers choose an Employee
of the Month or recommend
employees who give special service
or treatment.

198

Save the best parking space for
the Employee of the Month.

199

Choose an Employee of the Quarter and Year and give extra special bonuses and awards.

200

Have an annual recognition dinner
to thank everyone for a job well
done. Make a speech and thank
each person individually, by
department or as a group. Give
bonuses or plaques.

♥ ♥ ♥

201

When someone retires, give a gold watch, a party or a bonus. Let them know that they were appreciated and will be missed.

202

Give a round of applause.

203

Give a thank you and a handshake for a job well done. (In some industries or circumstances, even a hug can be appropriate!)

♥ ♥ ♥

204

Tell them they're the best!

205

Above all, remember the Golden Rule. Use common sense and compassion as your guide, and treat everyone with the courtesy, respect, and understanding that you would want.